My State
MISSOURI

By Christina Earley

TABLE OF CONTENTS

A Crabtree Seedlings Book

Crabtree Publishing
crabtreebooks.com

School-to-Home Support for Caregivers and Teachers

This book helps children grow by letting them practice reading. Here are a few guiding questions to help the reader build his or her comprehension skills. Possible answers appear in red.

Before Reading:

- What do I know about Missouri?
    - *I know that Missouri is a state.*
    - *I know that Missouri has the Gateway Arch.*

- What do I want to learn about Missouri?
    - *I want to learn which famous people were born in Missouri.*
    - *I want to learn what the state flag looks like.*

During Reading:

- What have I learned so far?
    - *I have learned that Jefferson City is the state capital of Missouri.*
    - *I have learned that the Gateway Arch is 630 feet (192 m) tall.*

- I wonder why...
    - *I wonder why the state flower is the white hawthorn blossom.*
    - *I wonder why there are so many fountains in Kansas City.*

After Reading:

- What did I learn about Missouri?
    - *I have learned that you can see stalagmites in Fisher Cave.*
    - *I have learned that the state animal is the Missouri mule.*

- Read the book again and look for the glossary words.
    - *I see the word **capital** on page 6, and the word **stalagmites** on page 20. The other glossary words are found on pages 22 and 23.*

MISSOURI
Hi! My name is Bennet. Welcome to Missouri!

I live in Kansas City. There are a lot of **fountains** in my city.

Kansas City is known for its tasty barbecue!

Missouri is in the **midwestern** United States. The **capital** is Jefferson City.

Fun Fact: Kansas City is the largest city in Missouri.

The state animal is the Missouri mule.

The white hawthorn blossom is the state flower.

We grow a lot of soybeans in Missouri. Some of them are used to make soy sauce.

Fun Fact: Missouri is one of the states that **produces** the most soybeans in the U.S.

My state flag has red, white, and blue stripes. The state **coat of arms** is in the middle.

My family likes to watch the Kansas City Chiefs play football.

I like to visit the Gateway Arch in St. Louis. We can see the Mississippi River from the top.

Fun Fact: The Gateway Arch is 630 feet (192 m) tall.

I enjoy boating on Lake of the Ozarks.

My family and I ride roller coasters at Silver Dollar City.

Poet Maya Angelou was born in Missouri. Ballet dancer Misty Copeland was also born in Missouri.

Fun Fact: President Harry S. Truman was born in Lamar, Missouri.

I like to see **stalagmites** in Fisher Cave.

I enjoy skiing at Hidden Valley.

Glossary

capital (cap-ih-tuhl): The city or town where the government of a country, state, or province is located

coat of arms (coht uv armz): A special group of pictures, usually shown on a shield

fountain (foun-tin): A structure that shoots streams of water into the air

midwestern (mid-west-urn): The northern central part of the United States

produces (pruh-doos-es): Makes or grows something for sale or use

stalagmites (stuh-lag-mahyts): Pointed pieces of rock that rise from a cave floor and that are formed by dripping water which contains minerals

Index

About the Author

Christina Earley lives in sunny South Florida with her husband and son. She enjoys traveling around the United States and learning about different historical places. Her hobbies include hiking, yoga, and baking.

Written by: Christina Earley
Designed and Illustrated by: Bobbie Houser
Series Development: James Earley
Proofreader: Melissa Boyce
Educational Consultant: Marie Lemke M.Ed.

Photographs:
Alamy: Yvette Cardozo: p. 17; ZUMA Press, Inc.: p. 18 left
Newscom: Jason Pohuski/Cal Sport Media: p. 13
Shutterstock: Charles Knowles: cover; Latecia Peoples: p. 3; Wallace Weeks: p. 4, 22; Michelle Lee Photography: p. 5; Volina: p. 6, 22-23; Sean Pavone: p. 7, 14-15; Marie-Jamieson: p. 8; sebastianosecondi: p. 9; oticki: p. 10-11; Fotokostic: p. 11, 23; railway fx: p. 12, 22; Hendrickson Photography: p. 14; Water Street: p. 16; Featureflash Photo Agency: p. 18 right; Lindasj22: p. 20, 23; schankz: p. 21
whitehouse.gov: p. 19

Crabtree Publishing

crabtreebooks.com 800-387-7650

Printed in the U.S.A./072023/CG20230214

Published in Canada
Crabtree Publishing
616 Welland Avenue
St. Catharines, Ontario
L2M 5V6

Published in the United States
Crabtree Publishing
347 Fifth Avenue
Suite 1402-145
New York, New York, 10016

Library and Archives Canada Cataloguing in Publication
Available at Library and Archives Canada

Library of Congress Cataloging-in-Publication Data
Available at the Library of Congress

Hardcover: 978-1-0398-0522-4
Paperback: 978-1-0398-0554-5
Ebook (pdf): 978-1-0398-0618-4
Epub: 978-1-0398-0586-6